by Iain Gray

Lang**Syne**

PUBLISHING

WRITING *to* REMEMBER

WRITING *to* REMEMBER

79 Main Street, Newtongrange,
Midlothian EH22 4NA
Tel: 0131 344 0414   Fax: 0845 075 6085
E-mail: info@lang-syne.co.uk
www.langsyneshop.co.uk

Design by Dorothy Meikle
Printed by Printwell Ltd
© Lang Syne Publishers Ltd 2019

ISBN 978-1-85217-509-2

Wilkinson

MOTTO:

Hold the right *(and)*

Neither for king nor people, but for both *(and)*

To be and to seem to be *(and)*

I persevere in what I undertake *(and)*

Glory to thee, not to me.

CREST:

A unicorn emerging from a crown.

NAME variations include:

Wilkenson

Wilkennson

Wilkieson

Wilkie

Wilkins

Chapter one:

The origins of popular surnames

by George Forbes and Iain Gray

If you don't know where you came from, you won't know where you're going is a frequently quoted observation and one that has a particular resonance today when there has been a marked upsurge in interest in genealogy, with increasing numbers of people curious to trace their family roots.

Main sources for genealogical research include census returns and official records of births, marriages and deaths – and the key to unlocking the detail they contain is obviously a family surname, one that has been 'inherited' and passed from generation to generation.

No matter our station in life, we all have a surname – but it was not until about the middle of the fourteenth century that the practice of being identified by a particular surname became commonly established throughout the British Isles.

Previous to this, it was normal for a person to be identified through the use of only a forename.

But as population gradually increased and there were many more people with the same forename, surnames were adopted to distinguish one person, or community, from another.

Many common English surnames are patronymic in origin, meaning they stem from the forename of one's father – with 'Johnson,' for example, indicating 'son of John.'

It was the Normans, in the wake of their eleventh century conquest of Anglo-Saxon England, a pivotal moment in the nation's history, who first brought surnames into usage – although it was a gradual process.

For the Normans, these were names initially based on the title of their estates, local villages and chateaux in France to distinguish and identify these landholdings.

Such grand descriptions also helped enhance the prestige of these warlords and generally glorify their lofty positions high above the humble serfs slaving away below in the pecking order who had only single names, often with Biblical connotations as in Pierre and Jacques.

The only descriptive distinctions among the peasantry concerned their occupations, like 'Pierre the swineherd' or 'Jacques the ferryman.'

Roots of surnames that came into usage in England not only included Norman-French, but also Old French, Old Norse, Old English, Middle English, German, Latin, Greek, Hebrew and the Gaelic languages of the Celts.

The Normans themselves were originally Vikings, or 'Northmen', who raided, colonised and eventually settled down around the French coastline.

The had sailed up the Seine in their longboats in 900AD under their ferocious leader Rollo and ruled the roost in north eastern France before sailing over to conquer England in 1066 under Duke William of Normandy – better known to posterity as William the Conqueror, or King William I of England.

Granted lands in the newly-conquered England, some of their descendants later acquired territories in Wales, Scotland and Ireland – taking not only their own surnames, but also the practice of adopting a surname, with them.

But it was in England where Norman rule and custom first impacted, particularly in relation to the adoption of surnames.

This is reflected in the famous *Domesday Book*, a massive survey of much of England and Wales, ordered by William I, to determine who owned what, what it was worth and therefore how much they were liable to pay in taxes to the voracious Royal Exchequer.

Completed in 1086 and now held in the National Archives in Kew, London, 'Domesday' was an Old English word meaning 'Day of Judgement.'

This was because, in the words of one contemporary chronicler, "its decisions, like those of the Last Judgement, are unalterable."

It had been a requirement of all those English landholders – from the richest to the poorest – that they identify themselves for the purposes of the survey and for future reference by means of a surname.

This is why the *Domesday Book*, although written in Latin as was the practice for several centuries with both civic and ecclesiastical records, is an invaluable source for the early appearance of a wide range of English surnames.

Several of these names were coined in connection with occupations.

These include Baker and Smith, while Cooks, Chamberlains, Constables and Porters were to be found carrying out duties in large medieval households.

The church's influence can be found in names such as Bishop, Friar and Monk while the popular name of Bennett derives from the late fifth to mid-sixth century Saint Benedict, founder of the Benedictine order of monks.

The early medical profession is represented by Barber, while businessmen produced names that include Merchant and Sellers.

Down at the village watermill, the names that cropped up included Millar/Miller, Walker and Fuller, while other self-explanatory trades included Cooper, Tailor, Mason and Wright.

Even the scenery was utilised as in Moor, Hill, Wood and Forrest – while the hunt and the chase supplied names that include Hunter, Falconer, Fowler and Fox.

Colours are also a source of popular surnames, as in Black, Brown, Gray/Grey, Green and White, and would have denoted the colour of the clothing the person habitually wore or, apart from the obvious exception of 'Green', one's hair colouring or even complexion.

The surname Red developed into Reid, while

Blue was rare and no-one wanted to be associated with yellow.

Rather self-important individuals took surnames that include Goodman and Wiseman, while physical attributes crept into surnames such as Small and Little.

Many families proudly boast the heraldic device known as a Coat of Arms, as featured on our front cover.

The central motif of the Coat of Arms would originally have been what was borne on the shield of a warrior to distinguish himself from others on the battlefield.

Not featured on the Coat of Arms, but high-lighted on page three, is the family motto and related crest – with the latter frequently different from the central motif.

Adding further variety to the rich cultural heritage that is represented by surnames is the appearance in recent times in lists of the 100 most common names found in England of ones that include Khan, Patel and Singh – names that have proud roots in the vast sub-continent of India.

Echoes of a far distant past can still be found in our surnames and they can be borne with pride in commemoration of our forebears.

Chapter two:

On the field of battle

A name found throughout the British Isles since at least the late eleventh century, 'Wilkinson' and its several spelling variants is a name of truly warlike origin.

Meaning 'son of Wilkin', it derives from the popular forename of 'William', which in turn has roots in the Germanic 'will', indicating 'fierce determination' and 'helm', meaning 'armed.'

In common with many other popular English surnames of today, it was first introduced to British shores in the wake of the Norman Conquest of 1066.

By this date, England had become a nation with several powerful competitors to its Anglo-Saxon throne. In what were extremely complex family, political and military machinations, the monarch was Harold II, who had succeeded to the throne following the death of Edward the Confessor.

But his right to the throne was contested by two powerful competitors – his brother-in-law King Harold Hardrada of Norway, in alliance with Tostig, Harold II's brother, and Duke William II of Normandy.

In what has become known as The Year of Three Battles, Hardrada invaded England and gained victory over the English king on September 20th at the battle of Fulford, in Yorkshire.

Five days later, however, Harold II decisively defeated his brother-in-law and brother at the battle of Stamford Bridge.

But Harold had little time to celebrate his victory, having to immediately march south from Yorkshire to encounter a mighty invasion force, led by Duke William of Normandy that had landed at Hastings, in East Sussex.

Harold's battle-hardened but exhausted force confronted the Normans on October 14.

It was at the top of Senlac Hill that Harold drew up a strong defensive position, building a shield wall to repel Duke William's cavalry and infantry.

The Normans suffered heavy losses, but through a combination of the deadly skill of their archers and the ferocious determination of their cavalry they eventually won the day.

Anglo-Saxon morale had collapsed on the battlefield as word spread through the ranks that Harold had been killed.

William was declared King of England on

December 25, and the complete subjugation of his Anglo-Saxon subjects followewd. Those Normans who had fought on his behalf, including those who bore what would become the name of Wilkinson, were rewarded with the lands of Anglo-Saxons.

It was in the north of England, particularly the area of present day Co. Durham, that the Wilkinson name first began to predominate.

This was through the descendants of a Norman knight who, as reward for his services to William the Conqueror, was granted lands in the Welsh area of Glamorgan. The family not only prospered in Wales, but also acquired lands in Co. Durham.

But the name also came to be found in areas far removed from the north of England – with a Roger Wyleconsecone, for example, recorded in Sussex in 1332.

The proud name of Wilkinson figures prominently not only in the frequently bloody historical record of England but also that of other nations.

A lieutenant in the army of the ill-fated Charles I, Laurence Wilkinson paid dearly for his loyalty to the Stuart monarch by having his north of England estates sequestered and sold by the victorious Parliamentary regime of Oliver Cromwell.

King of England, Scotland and Ireland from 1625 until his execution, Charles had incurred the wrath of Parliament by his insistence on the 'divine right' of monarchs. Added to this was Parliament's fear of Catholic 'subversion' against the state and the king's stubborn refusal to grant demands for religious and constitutional concessions.

Matters came to a head with the outbreak of the English Civil War in 1642, with Parliamentary forces, known as the New Model Army and commanded by Oliver Cromwell and Sir Thomas Fairfax, arrayed against the Royalist army of the king.

In what became an increasingly bloody and complex conflict, spreading to Scotland and Ireland and with rapidly shifting loyalties on both sides, the 49-year-old king was eventually captured and executed in January of 1649 on the orders of Parliament.

Five years earlier, Lieutenant Wilkinson had been taken prisoner when the royalist enclave of Newcastle was forced to surrender. Through a special dispensation of Parliament, he was allowed to move with his family in 1652 to New England, settling in Providence, Rhode Island.

It was here that he died in 1692.

In later centuries, bearers of the Wilkinson

name were to be found on other fields of battle – with many gaining honours and distinction.

No fewer than four bearers of the name were recipients of the Victoria Cross (VC), the highest award for valour in the face of enemy action for British and Commonwealth forces.

Born in 1896 in Leigh, Lancashire, Alfred Wilkinson was an English recipient of the honour during the First World War.

He had been a private in the 1/5th Battalion, The Manchester Regiment, when in October of 1918 at Marou, France, he braved heavy enemy shell and machine-gun fire to take an urgent message back from the front-line to his unit's supporting company. Later promoted to the rank of lieutenant, he died in 1940 as a result of a mining accident in his native Lancashire.

No fewer than three bearers of the name 'Thomas Wilkinson' were also recipients of the VC.

Born in 1831 in York, it was during the Crimean War of 1853 to 1856 that Bombardier Thomas Wilkinson won his VC. It was while serving as a bombardier in the Royal Marine Artillery that in June of 1855, at Sebastopol, he worked under fierce enemy fire to repair vital defences.

Later promoted to the rank of sergeant

instructor, he died in 1887, while his VC is now on display at the Royal Marines Museum, Southsea.

Born in 1894 in Shropshire, Lieutenant Thomas Wilkinson was a First World recipient of the VC. Immigrating to Canada with his family, he joined the 16th Battalion, Canadian Scottish, on the outbreak of the conflict in 1914.

Later transferred as a lieutenant with the 7th Battalion, the Loyal North Lancashire Regiment as a gunnery officer, it was in July of 1916 at La Boiselle, France, that he performed the deed for which he was posthumously awarded the honour.

He was killed after single-handedly manning a machine-gun to repel an enemy attack and later attempting to rescue a wounded comrade. His VC is now on display at the Imperial War Museum, London.

At sea, Lieutenant Thomas Wilkinson, born in 1898 in Widnes, Lancashire, was a posthumous Second World War recipient of the VC.

Serving with the Royal Naval Reserve, he was in command of the patrol vessel *Li Wo* in February of 1942 in the Java Sea, off Malaya.

Sighting two Japanese convoys, escorted by warships, he decided to engage them.

He and his crew managed to destroy one

enemy transport before *Li Wo* was hit at point-blank range with shell fire from a heavy cruiser.

Lieutenant Wilkinson went down with his stricken vessel, after having ordered his crew to abandon ship.

In the dark world of clandestine warfare, Peter Wilkinson, born in India in 1914, was the British army officer who served during the Second World War as a member of the Special Operations Executive (SOE) – the secret unit that specialised in daring acts of espionage, sabotage and assassination in Nazi-occupied Europe.

Serving for a time after the war as Co-ordinator of Intelligence in the Cabinet Office and later knighted, he also served from 1966 to 1967 as British Ambassador to Vietnam; he died in 2000.

Professor of International Relations and former director of the University of St Andrews Centre for the Study of Terrorism and Political Violence, Paul Wilkinson was born in 1937 in Harrow, Middlesex.

An adviser to the British Government on the scourge of terrorism, before his death in 2011 he published books that include the 1974 *Political Terrorism*, the 1989 *Lessons from Lockerbie* and his 1995 *Combating International Terrorism*.

Chapter three:

Enterprise and invention

Far from the fields of international warfare and terrorism, bearers of the Wilkinson name have stamped a distinctive mark on the historical record through a range of more peaceful pursuits.

One particularly enterprising and colourful bearer of the name was the eighteenth century English industrialist John Wilkinson.

Also known by his nickname of "Iron-Mad" Wilkinson, it was during the Industrial Revolution that he pioneered the manufacture and use of cast iron.

Born in 1728 in Little Clifton, in what is now the northern English region of Cumbria, his father Isaac worked at a nearby blast furnace.

Apprenticed to a Liverpool merchant for five years, John Wilkinson was aged 22 when he entered into an iron-making partnership with his father at the Bersham blast furnace near Wrexham.

His fortunes rapidly flourished, as he

established iron works throughout Shropshire and at Bilston, near Wolverhampton.

It was at his Bradley works in Bilston that he successfully utilised raw coal as a substitute for coke in the production of cast iron.

As his iron manufacturing empire expanded throughout England, Wilkinson in 1774 patented a technique for boring iron guns and cannon from a solid piece, while he also invented a technique for accurately boring cylinders for use in steam engines.

Producer by 1796 of about one eighth of Britain's cast iron and by then having earned his nickname of "Iron-Mad" Wilkinson, he made elaborate arrangements before his death in 1808 to be buried in a cast iron coffin on his estate at Lindale, Lancashire –with a cast iron obelisk to mark the spot.

He left a vast fortune – but squabbling among his heirs and resultant legal bills meant that much of it was dissipated only twenty years after his death.

For reasons that remain unclear, his corpse and cast iron coffin were re-interred in other locations over the years.

The location of his final resting place is now unknown – but his cast iron obelisk remains at its original location.

Two nineteenth century bearers of the Wilkinson name were noted English architects.

Born in 1814 in Witney, Oxfordshire, George Wilkinson was aged 21 when he won a competition to design a workhouse that today now forms part of the campus of Oxford and Cherwell Valley College.

He then went on to design a further 24 workhouses in England, while in 1839 he was appointed architect for the Poor Law Commission in Ireland.

In addition to designing railway stations in Ireland that include Dublin's Harcourt Street Station, in 1845 he also published his *Practical Geology and Ancient Architecture of Ireland*.

A Fellow of the Royal Institute of British Architects, he died in 1890.

He was the older brother of the equally noted British Gothic Revival Architect William Wilkinson.

Born in Oxford in 1819, it was in Oxford that he carried out most of his major projects – including the famed Randolph Hotel, completed in 1864.

Also responsible for building a library for the Oxford Union and a number of schools, he died in 1901.

An 'architect' on a decidedly much less smaller scale, was Major Sir Nevile Wilkinson.

Not only a British Army officer but also a genealogist, he is however best known as a designer of dollhouses.

It was in 1908 that he was appointed Ulster King of Arms, Principal Herald of Ireland – responsible for the scrutiny, use and granting of Coats of Arms relating to Irish heraldry.

The last person to hold the post until it lapsed following his death in 1940 at the age of 71, his other passion was the design of dollhouses. The most famous of these are Pembroke Palace, completed in 1907, and Titania's Palace, completed in 1922.

The latter is now owned by the Legoland theme park in Windsor, Berkshire, while the other is housed at Wilton House, seat of the Earl of Pembroke.

Recognised as "The Father of British Egyptology", Sir John Gardner Wilkinson was born in 1797 in Little Missenden, Buckinghamshire.

It was his clergyman father who fired his enthusiasm for antiquities, and in 1819 he resolved to study Egyptology.

Aged 24 when he first arrived in Egypt, he remained there for twelve years, visiting all the known ancient sites and taking meticulous notes in addition to painstakingly recording inscriptions.

Dogged with ill-health, he had to return to England in 1833 and, two years after being elected to the scientific think-tank the Royal Society, published his *The Topography of Thebes and General View of Egypt*, followed two years later by his highly acclaimed three-volume *Manners and Customs of the Ancient Egyptians*.

This exhaustive work earned him a knighthood, and he made several other trips to Egypt up until 1855.

He died in 1875, while his collection of papers is held in the Bodleian Library, Oxford.

In the sciences, Sir Geoffrey Wilkinson was the Nobel Prize-winning English chemist born in 1921 in Tordmorden, Yorkshire.

The son of a house painter and a cotton mill worker, he furthered his education through winning scholarships.

Graduating in 1941 from Imperial College, London, he was later recruited along with other young chemists to work on a nuclear energy project in Canada.

Later based at Harvard University and then Imperial College, he was involved in pioneering research in the field of inorganic chemistry.

This culminated in the Nobel Prize for Chemistry in 1973, along with fellow chemist Ernst Otto Fischer; he died in 1996.

In the often cut-throat world of politics, one particularly feisty bearer of the Wilkinson name was Ellen Wilkinson, known to her contemporaries as "Red Ellen" because of her fiery red hair and left-wing politics.

Standing at just less than 5ft. in height, she nevertheless was a figure of imposing stature in early twentieth century British politics.

Born in 1891 in Ardwick, Manchester, the daughter of a textile worker, it was through winning a number of scholarships that she was able to attend Manchester University, later obtaining a degree in history.

Having joined the Independent Labour Party (ILP) at the age of 16, in 1920 she became a founding member of the Communist Party of Great Britain – but later left the party in favour of the Labour Party.

Elected to the House of Commons in 1924 as one of Britain's first female Members of Parliament (MPs), she represented the constituency of Middlesbrough East and later the equally economically depressed northern English constituency of Jarrow.

It was in 1936 that she organised the famous Jarrow march of 200 unemployed workers from Jarrow to London to present a petition for jobs to Parliament.

Appointed to the Second World War coalition government of Winston Churchill, in collaboration with Home Secretary Herbert Morrison she was responsible for the introduction of air raid shelters.

Appointed Minister of Education in the wake of the 1945 General Election, she saw the implementation of a radical Education Act and also successfully fought for the introduction of free school milk for children.

Her life was tragically cut short at the age of 55 when she died from an overdose of barbiturates.

Although her death was officially recorded as accidental, other sources at the time asserted she had committed suicide – relating to problems with her then secret love affair with the married Herbert Morrison.

Chapter four:

On the world stage

Bearers of the Wilkinson name have excelled through a wide variety of pursuits, not least in the highly competitive world of sport.

Recognised as one of the world's top rugby union players, **Jonny Wilkinson** is the inside-centre and fly-half born in 1979 in Frimley, Surrey.

A former member of the England national team, he rose to fame between 2001 and 2003, scoring the winning drop goal in the last minute of extra time against Australia in the final of the 2003 Rugby World Cup.

He retired from international rugby union in 2011.

On the fields of European football, **Howard Wilkinson** is the English former winger and manager born in 1943 in Sheffield.

Playing for teams that include Sheffield United, Sheffield Wednesday and Boston United, he was manager of Leeds United when the team won the 1992 First Division championship.

Caretaker manager of the England national

team in both 1999 and 2000, he also managed teams that include Notts County and Sunderland.

He is the father of the midfielder **Ben Wilkinson**, born in Sheffield in 1987 and who has played for teams that include Hull City, Gretna, Chester City and Boston United.

In Australia, **Alexander Wilkinson** is the central defender who has played for teams that include the A-League Central Coast Mariners.

Bearers of the Wilkinson name have also achieved fame on the fields of American football.

Born in 1916 in Minneapolis, Charles Burnham Wilkinson, better known as **Bud Wilkinson**, was not only a player and coach but also a broadcaster and a politician.

It was while the former Minnesota quarter-back was coach at the University of Oklahoma, that its team the Oklahoma Sooners won the national championship in 1950, 1955 and 1956.

Retiring from coaching in 1963, he ran unsuccessfully a year later as a Republican candidate for the U.S. Senate.

Later becoming a broadcaster for ABC Sports, he returned to coaching in 1978 with the St Louis Cardinals.

An inductee of the College Hall of Fame, he died in 1994.

Born in 1973 in Dayton, Ohio, **Dan Wilkinson**, also known as "Big Daddy" Wilkinson, is the former college and professional defensive tackle who played 13 seasons in the National Football League (NFL) with teams that include the Cincinnati Bengals, Washington Redskins and Miami Dolphins.

An inductee of the Canadian Football Hall of Fame, **Tom Wilkinson** is the retired quarterback who gained fame during his time with the Edmonton Eskimos of the Canadian Football League (CFL).

Born in 1943, he was the winner of the CFL's Most Outstanding Player Award in 1974.

In water polo, **George Wilkinson**, born in 1879 and who died in 1946, was the player who won a gold medal as a member of the British team at the 1900 Paris, 1908 London and 1912 Stockholm Olympic Games.

Still in the water, **Laura Wilkinson** is the American former diver, born in Houston in 1977, who won a gold medal in women's diving at the 2000 Sydney and 2005 Montreal Olympics.

Both medals were for the 10-metres platform event.

In the Canadian national sport of ice hockey, **Neil Wilkinson** is the retired defence player who throughout the 1980s and 1990s played for teams that include the Minnesota North Stars, Winnipeg Jets and Pittsburgh Penguins.

Born in 1967 in Selkirk, Manitoba, he is an inductee of the Manitoba Hockey Hall of Fame.

From ice hockey to the popular sport of baseball, **James Wilkinson** was the pioneering American sports executive who in 1912 founded the multi-racial All Nations team in Des Moines, Iowa.

It was eight years later that he founded the Negro League baseball team.

Born in 1878 in Algona, Iowa, he was posthumously elected to the Baseball Hall of Fame following his death in 1964.

On the tennis court, **Chris Wilkinson** is the British former player who, after turning professional in 1989, represented his country at the 1992 Olympics in Barcelona.

Born in 1970 in Southampton, he now works as a tennis coach and tennis commentator.

Not only an American champion softball player but also a champion bowler, **Dot Wilkinson** was born in 1921.

Playing with the softball team The Ramblers from 1933 to 1965, she helped them win the national title in 1940, 1948 and 1949, while as a professional bowler she was the winner of the 1962 Women's International Bowling Queen's Tournament.

Inducted into the National Softball Hall of Fame and Museum in 1970, she was inducted twenty years later into the International Bowling Hall of Fame.

From softball and bowling to snooker, **Gary Wilkinson** is the English player who turned professional in 1987 at the age of 21 and went on to become the 1992 World Matchplay Champion.

Bearers of the Wilkinson name have also excelled, and continue to excel, in the world of the creative arts.

Born in 1978 in Leeds, **Tom Wilkinson** is the acclaimed British actor who was nominated for an Academy Award for his roles in the 2001 film *In the Bedroom* and the 2007 *Michael Clayton*.

Winner in 2009 of Golden Globe and Primetime Emmy Awards for Best Supporting Actor in a television mini-series for his role in *John Adam*, he and his wife the actress Diana Hardcastle also played the roles of Joe Kennedy and his wife Rose in the mini-series *The Kennedys*.

Best known to television audiences for her role from 1976 to 1981 as Viola Stapleton in the American soap *Guiding Light*, **Kate Wilkinson** was the actress of stage, television and film born in San Francisco in 1916.

With film credits that include the 1966 *Edge of Night*, she died in 1993.

In the contemporary world of film **Adrienne Wilkinson** is the American actress whose television credits include *Sweet Valley High*, *Xena: Warrior Princess*, *ER* and *Charmed*.

Born in 1977 in Missouri, she is also noted for her involvement in a number of charitable initiatives that include literacy programmes and children and animal welfare.

Behind the camera lens, **John Wilkinson** was the American sound engineer who won an Academy Award for his work on the 1986 film *Platoon*.

Born in 1920 in Hartford, Connecticut, he was also nominated for Academy Awards for the 1978 *Days of Heaven* and the 1981 *Outland*; he died in 2002.

From the stage to the world of music, **Amanda Wilkinson** is the Canadian country music singer who is not only a best-selling artist in her own right, but also one of the three family members of the equally popular country group The Wilkinsons.

Born in 1982 in Belleville, Ontario, she is a member of The Wilkinsons along with her father Steve and her brother Tyler.

The band won the Independent Group of the Year accolade at the 2007 Country Music Awards, following albums that include the 2000 *Here and Now* and the 2004 *Highway*.

Nominated in 2006 for Female Artist of the Year at the Canadian Country Music Awards, Amanda Wilkinson's solo albums include her 2005 self-titled *Amanda Wilkinson*.

In a much different musical genre, **Colm Wilkinson** is the Irish-born Canadian tenor who is best known for first playing the role of Jean Valjean in London's West End and on New York's Broadway in *Les Misérables*.

Born in Dublin in 1944 and also known professionally as C.T. Wilkinson, he represented Ireland in the 1978 Eurovision Song Contest, coming fifth with *Born to Sing*.

Born in 1958 in Stoke-on-Trent, **Kevin Wilkinson** was the drummer who played during the 1980s and 1990s for a number of successful British bands that include The League of Gentlemen, The Waterboys, China Crisis and Squeeze; he died in 1999.

From music to the equally creative world of the written word, **Alec Wilkinson** is the American author who has been on the staff of the *New Yorker* magazine since 1980.

Born in 1952, he is the author of books that include his 1980 *Midnights*, the 2003 *Mr Apology* and, from 2012, *The Ice Balloon*.

One of the leading lights, along with Dorothy Livesay and P.K. Page, of the 1940s' modernist movement in Canadian poetry, **Anne Wilkinson** (née Gibbons) was the poet born in 1910 in Toronto.

Recognised for works that include her 1951 collection *Counterpoint to Sleep* and the 1955 *The Hangman Hangs the Holly*, she died in 1961.

Born in 1963 and immigrating with her family at the age of 12 from Derby, **Carole Wilkinson** is the English-born Australian author best known for her series of books for children and young adults that include her 2003 *Dragonkeeper* – winner of a Children's Book Council of Australia Book of the Year Award.

In the world of art, **Mark Wilkinson** is the

British illustrator known for creating the art work for the albums of a number of bands.

Born in Windsor in 1952, he has illustrated covers for bands that include Marillion, Iron Maiden and The Who.

Truly reaching for the heavens, **David Todd Wilkinson**, born in 1935 in Hillsdale, Michigan, was the renowned American cosmologist who carried out pioneering research into cosmic microwave background radiation (CMB).

This relates to the theory of creation known as the Big Bang.

Professor of physics at Princeton University from 1965 until his death in 2002, he was the recipient of a number of prestigious awards that include the Princeton President's Award for Distinguished Teaching and the James Craig Watson Medal.